P9-DGW-949

AMITYVILLE PUBLIC LIBRARY

WHO MADE MY LUNCH?

FROM GRAPES TO JELLY

BY BRIDGET HEOS · ILLUSTRATED BY STEPHANIE FIZER COLEMAN

AMICUS ILLUSTRATED and **AMICUS INK**
are published by Amicus
P.O. Box 1329, Mankato, MN 56002
www.amicuspublishing.us

© 2018 Amicus. International copyright reserved in all
countries. No part of this book may be reproduced in
any form without written permission from the publisher.

**LIBRARY OF CONGRESS
CATALOGING-IN-PUBLICATION DATA**
Names: Heos, Bridget, author. | Coleman, Stephanie Fizer,
    illustrator. | Heos, Bridget. Who made my lunch?
Title: From grapes to jelly / by Bridget Heos ; illustrated by
    Stephanie Fizer Coleman.
Description: Mankato, MN : Amicus, [2018] | Series: Who
    made my lunch?
Identifiers: LCCN 2016058348 (print) | LCCN 2017000278
    (ebook) | ISBN 9781681511221 (library binding) | ISBN
    9781681512129 (ebook) | ISBN 9781681521473 (pbk.)
Subjects: LCSH: Jelly—Juvenile literature. | Grapes—Juvenile
    literature. | Grape products—Juvenile literature.
Classification: LCC TX612.J4 H46 2018 (print) | LCC TX612.J4
    (ebook) | DDC 641.3/48—dc23
LC record available at https://lccn.loc.gov/2016058348

EDITOR: Rebecca Glaser

DESIGNER: Kathleen Petelinsek

Printed in the United States of America
HC 10 9 8 7 6 5 4 3 2
PB 10 9 8 7 6 5 4 3 2 1

ABOUT THE AUTHOR
Bridget Heos is the author of more than 80 books
for children. She lives in Kansas City with her
husband and four children. Her favorite toast
topping is plum preserves.

ABOUT THE ILLUSTRATOR
Stephanie Fizer Coleman is an illustrator, tea
drinker, and picky eater from West Virginia, where
she lives with her husband and two silly dogs. When
she's not drawing, she's getting her hands dirty in the
garden or making messes in the kitchen.

Nothing sweetens up a peanut butter sandwich like grape jelly. But what if you had to make the jelly yourself? And you also had to grow the grapes?

Grapes for jelly can grow anywhere with warm days,
cool nights, and cold winters. Concord grapes are
the most common type for making jelly.

In early spring, find a big sunny field. You won't plant
seeds. Instead, buy vines from a plant nursery. Dig
holes for the vines. Build a trellis for them to grow on.

Water the vines and watch them grow. Unfortunately, you can't let grapes grow this year, or next. These are baby vines. They're too small to hold the heavy grapes. Trim the vines before they bear fruit.

Now that the vines are big and strong,

you can let the grapes grow . . .

. . . and grow and grow. Wow! That's a lot of grapes. It will take you a long time to pick them! You could ask friends to help you.

Or you could use a grape harvester. Drive it over the trellis. Two rods shake the vines on either side. The grapes land in a tray. Fans and screens remove the leaves and twigs.

Quick, get the grapes to the jelly factory while they're still fresh!

At the jelly factory, the fruit must be inspected. Are the grapes the right color? They should be purplish blue. Are they ripe? Most importantly, are they delicious?

These grapes passed the test. They are washed. Then a machine crushes the grapes. The juice moves through a screen that catches the fruit pieces. For jam, both the juice and fruit chunks would be used. But jelly is made from juice only.

Next, the juice must be
heated and chilled to kill
bacteria. This keeps it
from spoiling. Now you
can make the jelly!

Pump the juice into a mixing vat. Add sugar and pectin, a chemical that thickens the jelly. Heat the vat. As it cooks, the jelly will slowly thicken.

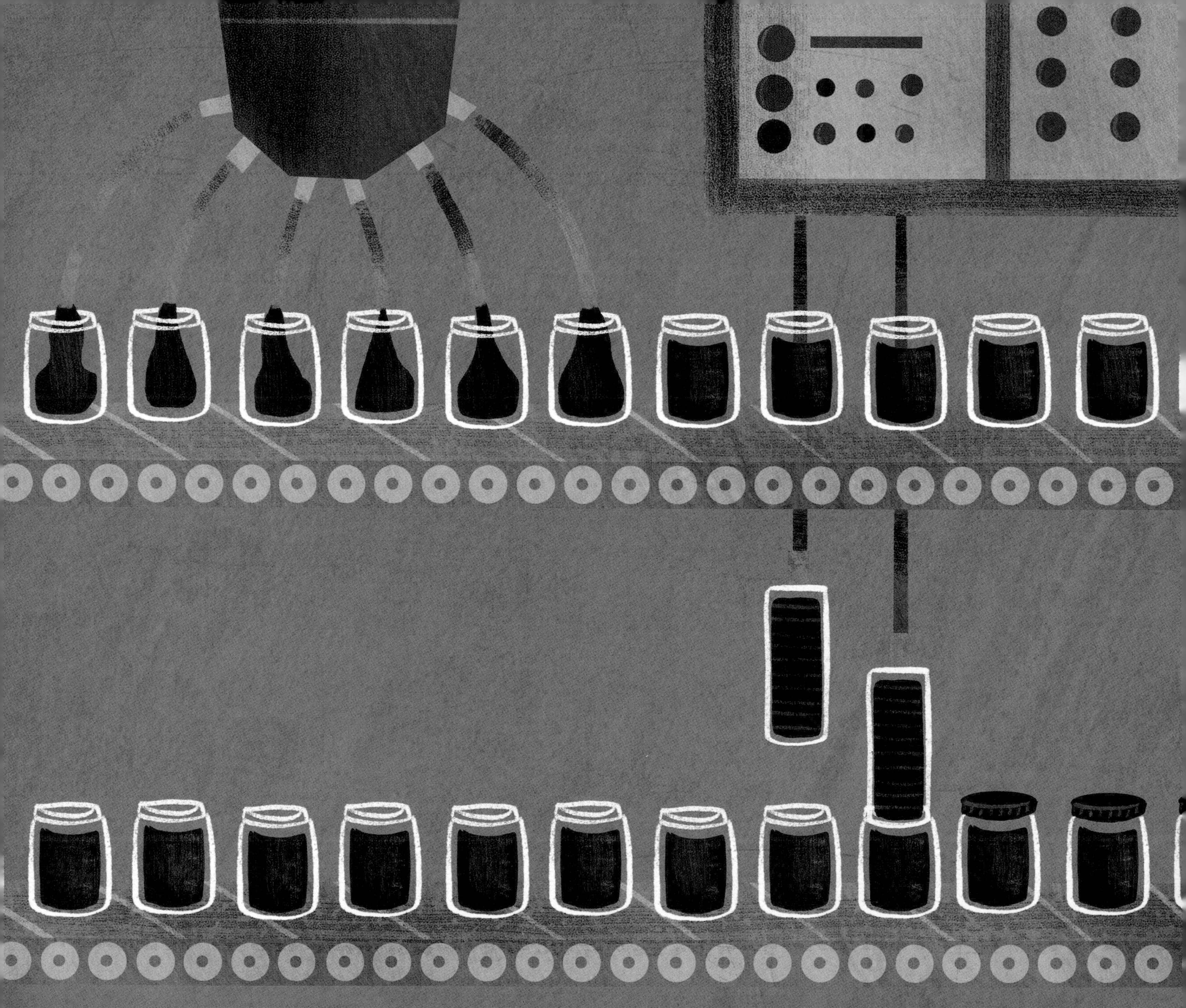

When the jelly is thick enough, pump it into the filling machine. Squirt! This machine fills many jelly jars at once. It screws on the caps and pastes on the labels. Then it drops the jars into boxes.

Before the jelly leaves the factory, each batch is tested. A jar is taken to the lab. A scientist makes sure it doesn't contain harmful bacteria. She also makes sure it tastes good. Yum, it does! Now, the jelly can be delivered to the store.

Thanks to the grape growers, jelly cooks, and factory inspectors, you can buy delicious jelly at the store. And don't forget the best part: eating the jelly! Yum!

WHERE ARE CONCORD GRAPES GROWN?

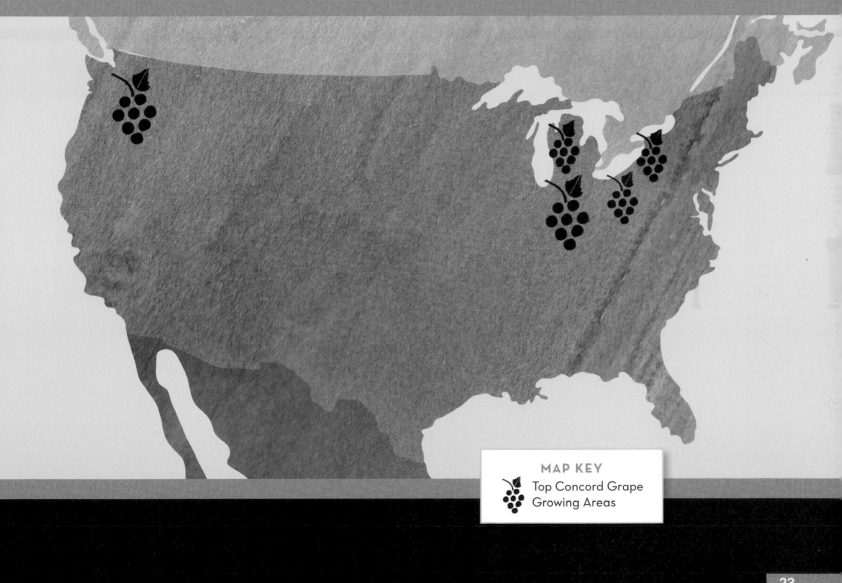

MAP KEY
Top Concord Grape Growing Areas

GLOSSARY

bacteria Microscopic, single-celled living things that can be either helpful or harmful.

harvester A machine that gathers crops that are ready for picking.

pectin A chemical that occurs naturally in fruit but is also added to jelly for thickening.

trellis A framework used to support growing plants.

vine A plant with a narrow stem that needs support and grows by winding around anything in its path.

WEBSITES

Fruit & Veggie Color Champions
http://foodchamps.org/
Play online games to learn about fruits and vegetables.

My First Garden
http://extension.illinois.edu/firstgarden/
Learn how to grow your own garden.

Super Healthy Kids
http://www.superhealthykids.com/ homemade-jam-even-a-child-could-make/
Make homemade jam with a grown-up's help.

Every effort has been made to ensure that these websites are appropriate for children. However, because of the nature of the Internet, it is impossible to guarantee that these sites will remain active indefinitely or that their contents will not be altered.

READ MORE

Nelson, Robin. *From Peanut To Peanut Butter.* Minneapolis: Lerner, 2013.

Nolan, Janet. *PB&J Hooray!: Your Sandwich's Amazing Journey from Farm to Table.* Chicago: Albert Whitman & Co., 2014.

Reynolds, Wendy A. *Turning Apples Into Applesauce.* New York: Cavendish Square Publishing, 2016.

29.95

AMITYVILLE PUBLIC LIBRARY

FEB 21 2018